Next Generation Physical Science and Everyday Thinking

Unit SE

Developing a Model for Static Electricity

Soda-can + tinsel   Acrylic   Styrofoam

Activate Learning®

Next Gen

PET LC

Lecture-style Class

Next Generation Physical Science and Everyday Thinking

Unit SE
Developing a Model for Static Electricity

Lecture-style Class

Major support for the development of *Next Gen PET* came from the National Science Foundation Grant No. 1044172 and the Chevron Corporation

© 2018 San Diego State University Research Foundation

human energy·

Activate Learning
44 Amogerone Crossway #7862
Greenwich, CT 06836
www.activatelearning.com

Next Generation Physical Science and Everyday Thinking (*Next Gen PET*)
© 2018 San Diego State University Research Foundation
Licensed exclusively to Activate Learning.

Printed and bound in the United States of America.

ISBN 978-1-68231-338-1
4th Printing
4 5   22 21 20

This project was supported, in part, by the National
Science Foundation under Grant No. 1044172. Opinions
expressed are those of the authors and not necessarily those
of the National Science Foundation.

Next Gen PET Development Team

Co-authors of Next Gen PET

Fred Goldberg, San Diego State University
Stephen Robinson, Tennessee Technological University
Danielle Harlow, University of California at Santa Barbara
Julie Andrew, University of Colorado at Boulder
Edward Price, California State University at San Marcos
Michael McKean, San Diego State University

Contributed to Development of Materials

Valerie Otero, University of Colorado at Boulder
Paula Engelhardt, Tennessee Technological University
Rebecca Stober, University of Colorado at Boulder
Cary Sneider, Portland State University
Rebecca Kruse Vincent, National Science Foundation
Nephi Thompson, Colorado Mountain College
David Mitchell, California Polytechnic University at San Luis Obispo
Leslie Atkins, Boise State University

Field Test Collaborators

David Mitchell, California Polytechnic University at San Luis Obispo
Anne Marie Bergen, California Polytechnic University at San Luis Obispo
Lola Berber-Jimenez, California Polytechnic University at San Luis Obispo
Nancy Stauch, California Polytechnic University at San Luis Obispo
Tina Duran, California Polytechnic University at San Luis Obispo
Chance Hoellwarth, California Polytechnic University at San Luis Obispo
Paula Engelhardt, Tennessee Technological University

Technical Support

Shawn Alff, San Diego State University Katie
Badham, San Diego State University Megan
Santos, San Diego State University James
Powell, San Diego State University
Anne E. Leak, University of California at Santa Barbara
Noreen Balos, University of California at Santa Barbara
Leo Farias, California Polytechnic University at San Luis Obispo
Loren Johnson, California Polytechnic University at San Luis Obispo
Liz Walker, Tennessee Technological University
Ryan Calloway, Tennessee Technological University
Carla Moore, Tennessee Technological University
Ian Robinson, Tennessee Technological University
Rob Reab, Tennessee Technological University
Nate Reynolds, California State University at San Marcos
Lauran Gerhart, California State University at San Marcos

Unit SE: Developing a Model for Static Electricity
Table of Contents

---

[1] Extensions (Ext) are online, interactive homework activities.

Purpose and Materials Needed

In the previous unit you explored some magnetic effects and then went on to develop a model that explains these effects in terms of tiny entities within magnetic materials. You are also likely familiar with some other phenomena, usually associated with *static electricity*, like the 'static cling' by which clothes stick together when you remove them from a drier, or the 'shock' you receive when you walk across a carpet and then touch something. In this unit, you will develop another model to explain these effects associated with static electricity. To start, in this lesson you will observe some static electric effects and look for some patterns on which to base your initial model.

 What are some properties of interactions involving electrified objects?

For these investigations your team will need:

▶ Roll of sticky tape
▶ Pen or permanent marker
▶ A support, such as a ruler or long pencil
▶ An envelope containing several items

Predictions, Observations and Making Sense

Part 1: What kinds of materials can be involved in static electric effects?

In the previous unit you found that only certain materials could interact with a magnet. Will it be only these same materials that interact with electrified objects, or will different materials show static electric effects? What do you think?

CQ 1-1: What kinds of materials do you think can be involved in static electric effects?

A. All materials, both metals (copper, aluminum, iron, brass, etc.) and non-metals (plastic, wood, glass, etc.)
B. Only metals, but not non-metals
C. Only non-metals, but not metals
D. Only certain metals, not all metals
E. Only certain metals and non-metals, but not all of them

To find out, you will perform some experiments with electrified and non-electrified objects. You are no doubt aware that some objects can be electrified by rubbing them, but for these experiments you will use a different technique to electrify two pieces of sticky tape.

To begin, open the small envelope in your kit and lay out all the items (listed in Table I on the next page) on a desktop. Add two additional items that you will be testing.

Read through the following steps first, and then go through them quickly, but carefully. Static electricity effects sometimes wear off quickly, so if you don't observe any types of interactions you might consider re-electrifying the tapes. If you don't have the materials, watch the movie **USE L1 Movie 1**.

Prepare two pieces of sticky tape, each about 4 inches long. Fold over about $1/2$ inch of both ends of both pieces of sticky tape. These ends will serve as 'handles' that will allow you to work with the tape without touching the sticky surfaces.

Place one of the pieces of tape on the desk in front of you, sticky side down. Using a pen or other permanent marker, label one of the handles on this piece B (for Bottom).

Now place a second piece of tape directly on top of the first, again sticky side down. Label this piece T (for Top).

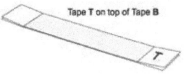

Tape T on top of Tape B

Rub you finger over the two pieces to make sure they are firmly stuck together. (The bottom piece will also be stuck to the table, but that is not important.)

One member of your group should slowly peel both pieces of tape, still stuck together, from the table. (If the two pieces of tape become separated press them firmly together again.)

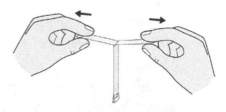

Holding a handle on each piece of tape in each hand, quickly rip them apart. Keep your two hands far apart so the tapes do not touch. [Ripping the tapes apart should electrify each of them.]

To find out how the various materials in your envelope interact with the electrified tapes, *other members of your group should slowly bring each item close to each of the two tapes in turn. Do this quickly.* As soon as any reaction from the tape is observed, pull the object away again. Try not to let the tape touch any of the objects. Without the materials, you should watch the movie [**USE L1 Movie 2**].

For each item, record in the table whether the tape is attracted (A) to it, repelled (R) from it, or there is no effect (O). Add two other items of your own choice to the table and test them. Finally, bring the tip of your finger close to each tape to see if there is any reaction.

Table I: Observations of Electrified Tapes near Objects (A, R or O)

	Wooden strip	Iron nail	Plastic pen/ruler	Aluminum foil strip	Copper wire	Nickel strip	Paper clip		Finger
T-tape									
B-tape									

What do your observations show about what types of materials can interact with electrified objects?

You can discard the two tapes. Your instructor will review the observations in the table and your conclusions to ensure that everyone agrees.

When Benjamin Franklin experimented with electrified objects, he imagined them as containing some type of electrical 'fluid' and so said they were 'charged' (as in 'charge [fill] your glasses for a toast') when describing them. While Franklin's use of 'charged' is probably different from the sense in which most people today think of it, we still use his terminology. Thus, from now on we will refer to electrified objects as being 'charged' with static electricity.

Part 2: How do electrically charged objects interact with each other?

In Part 1 you saw what happens when uncharged objects are brought near charged objects. But what would happen if two charged objects were brought near each other?

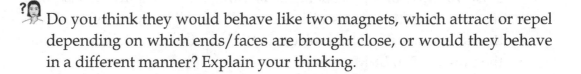 Do you think they would behave like two magnets, which attract or repel depending on which ends/faces are brought close, or would they behave in a different manner? Explain your thinking.

CQ 1-2: If different ends/faces of two electrically charged objects were brought close together, what do you think would happen?

A. It would be like two magnets. If they attracted each other when two of the ends/faces were close to each other, they would then repel if one of the ends/faces were turned around.
B. It would not be like two magnets. If two ends/faces attracted or repelled each other, they would do the same thing if one of the ends/faces were turned around.
C. They would not react to each other.

Two different experiments will help you check your thinking.

First, watch a movie (**USE L1 Movie 3**) of an experiment involving two plastic coffee stirrers. So that you can distinguish the ends, one end of each stirrer

will have a small piece of tape attached to it. One of the stirrers will be charged by rubbing it all over with wool, and then it will be placed on a floating disk.

The second stirrer will be charged in the same manner, and then both ends of it will be brought close to both ends of the floating charged stirrer.

🔍 Does what happens depend on which ends of the stirrers are tested, or does the same thing always happen regardless of the ends used?

🧩 How does this behavior of two wool-rubbed stirrers compare to the behavior of two magnet-rubbed nails you saw in Unit M?

The next experiment you will perform yourself. (If you do not have the materials, then watch **USE L1 Movie 4**.) Prepare a new pair of charged B and T tapes just as you did in Part 1. After ripping the B and T tapes apart, slowly bring them toward each other. As soon as you see any reaction, move them apart again. *It is important not to let the tapes touch each other!* (If they do, you should go through the whole charging process again!)

🔍 What happens as the B and T tapes approach each other? Do they attract, repel, or is there no reaction?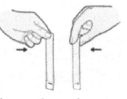

Turn one of the tapes around so its opposite side faces the other tape and bring the two tapes together again.

🔍 Do the results depend which ends/faces are tested, or does the same thing always happen?

In Unit M, you investigated what materials interact with a magnet and also whether magnetized objects are one-ended or two-ended.

🧩 Based on your observations in this lesson, what can you conclude: are charged objects one-ended or two-ended?

🧩 When compared with the results of your investigations in Unit M, do observations in this lesson suggest that the static electric and magnetic interactions are the same or different? Explain your reasoning.

Part 3: How many types of charge are there?

You have seen that during rubbing with wool, and the peeling apart of two tapes, objects involved become charged with static electricity. But is there only one type of charge, or are there more than one and if so, how many are there?

?👩 Suppose you prepared two pairs of charged tapes (call them T1/B1 and T2/B2) and brought tapes T1 and T2 together. What do you think would happen and why?

CQ 1-3: If the T1 and T2 tapes from two separate pairs of charged tapes were brought back toward each other, what do you think would happen?

    A. They would attract each other.
    B. They would repel each other.
    C. They would not react to each other.

Either perform the following experiment with the materials or watch a movie **(USE L1 Movie 5)** of the experiment. Prepare two pairs of B and T tapes so they are charged and label them B1, T1, B2, and T2. Then bring them toward each other in various combinations, as suggested in the following table.

Record the results of all the tests in Table II below. (Enter **A** for attract, **R** for repel, or **O** for no reaction.)

Table II: Observations with Charged Tapes

	B2	**T2**
B1		
T1		

What do the results from these experiments with charged tapes suggest about the number of types of charge involved and how they interact with each other?

Finally, we will check whether the ideas you have developed about charges using the pairs of tapes also apply to objects charged by rubbing them together.

Watch a movie (**USE L1 Movie 6**) of an experiment in which a Styrofoam plate and an acrylic sheet (a type of clear plastic) are rubbed together and each brought toward a pair of charged B and T tapes.

Describe how both tapes behave when the rubbed Styrofoam plate is brought near.

 Do these results suggest that the rubbed plate has the same type of charge as the B tape, the T tape, or some different type of charge?

🔍 Describe how both tapes behave when the rubbed acrylic sheet is brought near.

🧩 Do these results suggest that the rubbed acrylic sheet has the same type of charge as the B tape, the T tape, or some different type of charge?

Next, watch a movie (USE L1 Movie 7) that shows a rubber balloon being rubbed against a person's hair. Then the charged balloon is brought close to T and B tapes.

🔍 Describe how both tapes behave when the hair-rubbed balloon is brought near.

🧩 Do these results suggest that the hair-rubbed balloon has the same type of charge as the B tape, the T tape, or some different type of charge?

Summarizing Questions

S1. Use evidence from this lesson to answer the following question.

CQ 1-4: How many types of charge are there and how do they interact?
A. There is only one type of charge. All charged objects attract each other.
B. There is only one type of charge. All charged objects repel each other.
C. There are two types of charge. Like charges repel and unlike charges attract.
D. There are two types of charge. Like charges attract and unlike charges repel.

S2. Suppose you and your neighbors both rubbed a Styrofoam plate with an acrylic sheet and then brought the two plates together. What do you think would happen and why? What about if you brought your charged plate close to their charged acrylic sheet?

To get some feedback, watch the movie **USE L1 Movie 8**, which shows what happens when the two Styrofoam plates are brought together.

What actually happens?

S3. Answer the following question based on your current understanding of what happens when objects are charged by rubbing or peeling.

CQ 1-5: What happens when two objects are charged by rubbing or peeling?
  A. Both objects have the same type of charge.
  B. One object has only one type of charge. The other object has only the other type of charge.
  C. Both objects have both types of charge, but there are different amounts of each type on each object.

Purpose

In the previous unit, you developed and tested a model for magnetism that can account for what happens when a nail is rubbed with a magnet. In this lesson, you will begin the process of developing a *model for static electricity* that can account for how objects become charged with static electricity when they are rubbed together (or tapes pulled apart) and why they behave as they do when interacting with other objects, both charged and uncharged.

Note: While it would be good to obtain your evidence from experiments you do yourself, it is notoriously difficult to obtain consistent results with static electricity experiments in humid conditions like a classroom full of people. (You will consider why this might be in a later lesson.) Therefore, from now on you will mostly be making observations of experiments from videos made under controlled conditions.

> ### How can you construct a model of static electricity and use it to explain your observations?

Predictions, Observations and Making Sense

Part 1: What is your initial model for static electricity?

You know from the previous lesson that there seems to be two types of electric charge, just as there are two types of magnetic poles. However, you also saw that charged objects are *one-ended* (both sides or ends behave in the same way), whereas magnetized objects are *two-ended*. In representing magnetic materials, we used north (N) and south (S) symbols. However, because the two types of interaction are different in some way, we should use different symbols when representing charged materials. To make this distinction, we suggest you use positive (+) and negative (–) symbols in your models.

Using this convention, from the previous extension activity you concluded that when a Styrofoam plate is rubbed with an acrylic sheet, the acrylic sheet becomes positively (+) charged and the Styrofoam plate becomes negatively (–) charged.

Use the two drawings of the plate and sheet below to show your group's thinking, representing their states before and after they were charged. This represents your group's *initial model*.

Your group's initial model for rubbing two materials together:

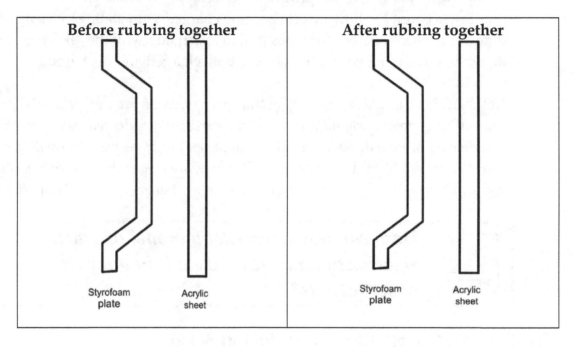

Describe your group's initial model in words, in particular how the "after rubbing" picture differs from the "before rubbing" picture. What do you think happens to the entities (if anything) while the plate and sheet are rubbed together?

Use your model to briefly explain the observation that *the Styrofoam and acrylic become oppositely charged when rubbed together, and that each of them is 'one-ended'*.

CQ 2-1: Which of the following best describes your initial model for what happens when the acrylic and Styrofoam are charged by rubbing them together?

A. Neither of the objects have any charged entities before rubbing together. During the rubbing, + charges are created on the acrylic, and – charges are created on the Styrofoam.

B. Before rubbing, both objects have equal numbers of + and – charges. During rubbing, charges are transferred so that the acrylic ends up with all the + charges and the Styrofoam ends up with all the – charges.

C. Before rubbing, both objects have equal numbers of + and – charges. During rubbing, some charges are transferred so that the acrylic ends up with more + charges than – charges, and the Styrofoam ends up with more – charges than + charges.

D. Before rubbing, both objects have equal numbers of + and – charges. During rubbing, extra + charges are created on the acrylic and extra – charges are created on the Styrofoam.

In the previous extension activity, you were also introduced to a simulation that represents positive charge with red coloring and negative charge with blue coloring. Watch a brief movie **(USE L2 Movie 1)** that simulates the acrylic sheet and Styrofoam being rubbed together. Notice the rubbed acrylic surface is colored red (+ charged) and the rubbed Styrofoam surface is colored blue (- charged).

Part 2: Touching charged and uncharged objects together

The experiments you will consider shortly use a device called an electroscope, made from an empty metal soda can taped to an upturned Styrofoam cup. Some loose strands of tinsel (which are effectively thin strips of metal) are hung from the ring-pull tab of the can so that the ends are free to move.

Watch a movie **(USE L2 Movie 2)** of an experiment in which a Styrofoam plate and acrylic sheet are first charged by rubbing them together. The + charged acrylic sheet then gently touches the tinsel on the electroscope and is pulled away again (they are **not** rubbed together). After this is done, the strands of tinsel are hanging in a **more 'spread out'** arrangement than before. Below are still frames from the movie.

Before: tinsel strands are close together   *After: tinsel strands are more spread out*

 After the + charged acrylic sheet touches the tinsel and is removed, do you think the tinsel is itself charged or not? If so, what type of charge does it have: the same as the acrylic sheet (+) or the opposite (-)? On the following diagrams, draw what +/– charged entities you think are inside or on the surface of the tinsel (if any), end of the soda can, and acrylic sheet before and after they have been in contact. Discuss your thinking with your group.

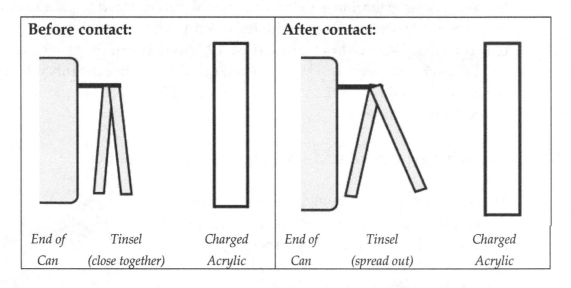

After the + charged acrylic touches the tinsel and is removed, does your model suggest the tinsel is now uncharged, + charged, or – charged?

How do your diagrams account for the observation that the strands of tinsel are hanging in a more 'spread out' arrangement after contact than before? (*Assume that the charged acrylic is too far away to directly affect the tinsel at these points in time.*)

You can check your ideas by making a prediction that can be tested. After the tinsel has touched the charged acrylic sheet, suppose first the + charged acrylic sheet and then the – charged Styrofoam plate were brought close to the tinsel again, **but not allowed to touch it.**

CQ 2-2: According to your model above, after the tinsel has touched the charged acrylic sheet, how would it react to the + charged acrylic and - charged Styrofoam?

    A. Attracted to the acrylic and repelled by the Styrofoam.
    B. Attracted to both the acrylic and the Styrofoam.
    C. Repelled by the acrylic and attracted to the Styrofoam.
    D. Repelled by both the acrylic and the Styrofoam.

Briefly explain your reasoning.

To get feedback, watch a movie **(USE L2 Movie 3)** of the experiment being performed.

Describe how the tinsel reacts (attracts, repels, no effect) to the:

    + charged acrylic sheet.

    – charged Styrofoam plate.

Based on your observations, what can you conclude about the charge state of the tinsel strands after they touched the charged acrylic sheet?

Did they have a positive (+) charge, a negative (-) charge, or no charge? How do you know?

Next, watch a movie **(USE L2 Movie 4)** from the simulation, representing what happens when the + charged acrylic touches the tinsel on the soda can. At the beginning of the movie, none of the objects are charged, but as it plays, charged areas will be represented by red (+) or blue (–) colors.

Based on your observations from the experiment and the simulation, discuss with your group whether your model needs to be revised. If so, re-draw it below. Remember to show what +/- charges, if any, are on the surface or inside the tinsel, end of soda can, and charged acrylic both before and after the acrylic touches the tinsel.

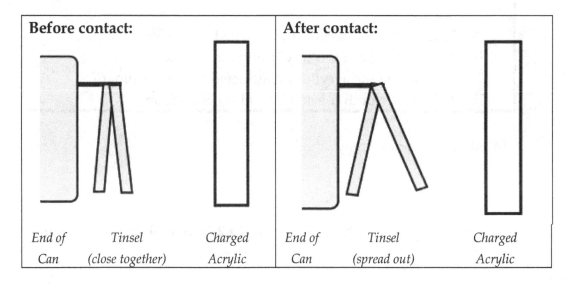

Before contact:			After contact:		
End of	*Tinsel*	*Charged*	*End of*	*Tinsel*	*Charged*
Can	*(close together)*	*Acrylic*	*Can*	*(spread out)*	*Acrylic*

Explain, in terms of the charged entitites involved, what you think happened when the tinsel touched the charged acrylic sheet.

Note: The behavior of the tinsel on an electroscope will serve as a tool in further experiments. If the tinsel is itself uncharged it will not react to an uncharged object, but it will be attracted toward any charged object, regardless of whether it is positively (+) or negatively (–) charged. (You know that there is always an attraction between charged and uncharged objects.) Thus, we can use it to check if an object is charged or not. If the tinsel becomes spread out, we know it is now charged and we can test what type of charge it has by using charged acrylic and Styrofoam.

Part 3: What happens when a charged object is touched all over with an uncharged object?

Watch a movie **(USE L2 Movie 5)** in which an experimenter rubs a plastic coffee stirrer with wool and then touches it all over with his fingers. To check whether the stirrer is charged or not at various points in the process, it will be brought close to the **uncharged tinsel** strands on a soda can electroscope.

Was the stirrer charged before it was rubbed with wool? What about after? How do you know?

Explain, in terms of the +/– charged entities involved in your model, what you think happened when the plastic stirrer was rubbed with the wool.

Now consider what happened when the experimenter touched the stirrer all over with his fingers.

Was the stirrer still charged after this was done? How do you know?

Explain, in terms of the +/– charged entitites involved in your model, what you think happened when the experimenter touched the plastic stirrer with his fingers.

CQ 2-3: Now imagine that after charging the stirrer with the wool, the experimenter immersed the stirrer in water and then removed it. If he brought the wet stirrer near the uncharged tinsel, what do you predict would happen?

A. The tinsel would be attracted to the wet stirrer.
B. The tinsel would be repelled from the wet stirrer.
C. The tinsel would not react to the wet stirrer.

Why do you think so?

Watch a movie (**USE L2 Movie 6**) of what actually happens.

What happened when the wet stirrer was brought near the tinsel?

Was the stirrer charged <u>after</u> it was immersed in water? How do you know?

If this result is not in agreement with your prediction, describe how your model might explain it in terms of the charged entities involved.

How might this result help explain why it is difficult to do static electricity experiments when there is a lot of humidity in the atmosphere?

Summarizing Questions

S1. You already know that **<u>two uncharged objects</u>** can be charged by rubbing them together (or peeling tapes apart).

CQ 2-4: What do your observations in this lesson suggest happens when an uncharged object touches a second object that is already charged?

    A. The uncharged object becomes charged in the same way as the second object.

    B. The uncharged object becomes charged in the opposite way as the second object.

    C. The uncharged object remains uncharged.

S2. Do your observations suggest that, in your model, you should regard the charged entities responsible for giving an object its overall charge as being inside the body of the object or on its surface? What evidence supports your answer?

Purpose

In the previous lesson you developed your initial model to account for static electric phenomena. It is common for most groups to have similar models for charged objects, associating arrangements of positively (+) and negatively (–) charged entities with them. However, there is often more variation in the model representations of uncharged objects (such as the acrylic sheet and Styrofoam plate before they were rubbed together), with some showing no entities, some showing neutral (uncharged) entities, and some showing equal numbers of + and – charged entities. The key question for this lesson is:

> *What is an appropriate way to represent uncharged objects in your model for static electricity?*

Predictions, Observations and Making Sense

Part 1: Bringing a charged object close to the electroscope

In the previous lesson you were introduced to a device called an electroscope, made from a soda can and some tinsel (thin metal strips). Suppose you had such a soda can electroscope that was **uncharged**. According to your current model, how would you represent this uncharged eleclectroscope?

 Use this diagram to show your thinking, drawing whatever entities (if any) you think necessary on both the can and the tinsel.

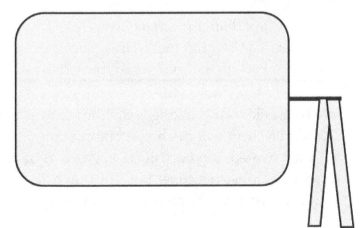

How does your diagram indicate that the soda can and tinsel are both uncharged? What evidence (if any) do you have to support this representation?

Part 2: Bringing a positively (+) charged object close to the uncharged electroscope

 Suppose you rubbed an acrylic sheet and a Styrofoam plate together to charge them, and then brought the positively (+) charged acrylic sheet close to (**but not touching**) the base of the uncharged electroscope you represented in Part 1. Do you think either the soda can or the tinsel would become electrically charged when this is done?

> **CQ 3-1:** If the charged acrylic sheet was brought close to the base of the can and then removed again (without touching the can), how do you think the tinsel strands at the other end of the can would behave?
>
> A. They would not react in any way.
> B. They would spread apart when the acrylic is near but then go back to 'normal' when it is removed.
> C. They would spread apart when the acrylic is near and stay spread apart after it is removed.
> D. They would move closer together when the acrylic is near but then go back to 'normal' when it is removed.

To check your thinking, watch the movie **USE L3 Movie 1**. In this movie an acrylic sheet will be charged by rubbing it with a Styrofoam plate. After this, the charged acrylic will be brought near to the base end of an uncharged soda-can electroscope, **but not touch it**, and then be moved further away again. This will be done a couple of times.

When the charged acrylic sheet is brought close to the other end of the soda can, does the tinsel become more spread out, more clumped together, or does it not show any reaction? What happens when the acrylic sheet is removed again?

Does this evidence support the conclusion that the <u>tinsel</u> is now *charged* or that it is *uncharged* when the charged acrylic is held nearby?

Work with your group to try and explain this behavior using your model, revising it if necessary.

Use the diagrams below to show how your current model now represents the objects involved (soda can, tinsel, and acrylic) before the charged acrylic is brought close, while it is close (with the tinsel spread out), and after it has been removed again.

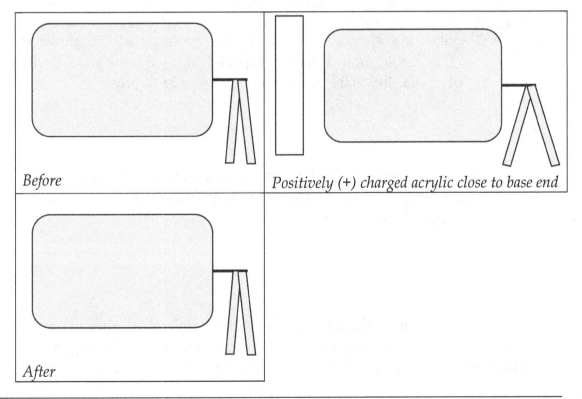

Before

Positively (+) charged acrylic close to base end

After

🧩 Explain how your model accounts for the behavior of the tinsel in terms of any entities involved.

You have now seen that when the positively (+) charged acrylic sheet is held close to the base end of the soda can electroscope, the tinsel at the other end becomes more spread out. From this you can infer that while the acrylic sheet is held in this position, the tinsel becomes charged, but was it positive (+) or negative (–)? Also, did the base end of the can become charged or not, and what happened to the charge on the acrylic?

To gather evidence to help address these questions, watch a movie **(USE L3 Movie 2)**. It shows the experimenter preparing two sets of charged acrylic and Styrofoam. He first holds one of the positively charged (+) acrylic sheets close to the base end of the uncharged electroscope, and the tinsel spreads out (as it did in the previous movie). Keeping the first positively (+) charged acrylic sheet close to the base end of the electroscope, he then brings the other positively (+) charged acrylic sheet close to the tinsel, followed by one of negatively (–) charged Styrofoam plates.

🔍 Describe how the tinsel reacts to the presence of the positively (+) charged acrylic. Is it attracted, repelled, or is there no reaction? What about its reaction to the negatively (–) charged Styrofoam?

🧩 When the positively (+) charged acrylic was held close to the base end of the uncharged electroscope, did the tinsel have a positive (+) or negative (–) charge? How do you know?

Next, watch a movie **(USE L3 Movie 3)** of a simulation of the situation where the acrylic and Styrofoam are rubbed together, and the charged acrylic is brought near (without touching) the base end of the soda can.

According to the simulation, when the positively (+) charged acrylic is brought close to one end of the simulator electroscope, does the tinsel at the other end become positively (+) or negatively (–) charged, or does it remain uncharged? How do you know?

While the positively (+) charged acrylic is held close to one side of the simulator electroscope, does that side of the electroscope (closest to the acrylic) become positively (+) or negatively (–) charged, or does it remain uncharged? How do you know?

After the positively (+) charged acrylic is moved away from the simulator electroscope, what happens to the charge states of the tinsel and the other end? Do they remain charged or do they become uncharged again? How do you know?

Based on your observations of the experiments and the simulation, your group should modify its model, if needed, to explain what happens when the positively (+) charged acrylic is brought near the base end of the electroscope.

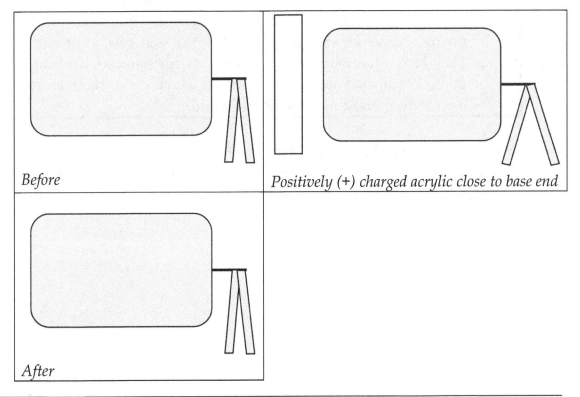

Before

Positively (+) charged acrylic close to base end

After

🧩 Briefly explain how the proximity of the positively (+) charged acrylic at the base end results in the tinsel end of the electroscope acquiring an an overall positive (+) charge and the base end an overall negative (–) charge.

As an extension activity to this lesson, you will explore what happens when a negatively (–) charged object is brought close to the uncharged electroscope.

Summarizing Questions

S1. Answer the following question based on the evidence you obtained during this lesson.

> **CQ 3-2:** Which of the following ideas about uncharged objects do you think it would it be most appropriate to include in your model?
>
> A. They have no electric entities associated with them. When such objects are involved in static electric interactions, + and – charged entities are created.
> B. They have neutral (uncharged) electric entities associate with them. When such objects are involved in static electric interactions, these neutral entities are changed into either + or – charged entities.
> C. They have equal numbers of + and – charged entities associated with them. When such objects are involved in static electric interactions, at least some of these entities move around.

S2. Use your model to explain why the tinsel on an uncharged electroscope goes back to hanging normally when a charged object is moved away from the other end. (You saw this happening at the end of the simulation movie **USE L3 Movie 3**.)

Purpose

You are currently developing a model for static electricity that involves the movement of +/− charged entities within and/or between objects. In this lesson, you will continue this development to account for how different materials behave when involved in static electricity effects.

 How can you refine your model to account for the behavior of metals and non-metals?

Predictions, Observations and Making Sense

Part 1: Can you charge an object without touching it directly?

In the previous lessons you saw that when some tinsel strands come into contact with a charged object, the tinsel itself becomes charged. In this lesson we will use two electroscopes, one made with a metal soda can as you saw in the previous lessons, and the second made with a plastic water bottle. Both are initially **uncharged**.

To begin, watch a movie **(USE L4 Movie 1)** of an experiment in which a positively (+) charged acrylic sheet is brought into **contact** with the **base end** of the soda can and water bottle on the uncharged electroscopes (the ends opposite the tinsel) for a few seconds, and then removed.

🔍 Describe what happens to the tinsel on each electroscope when this is done.

When the + charged acrylic sheet was touched to both electroscopes, did the tinsel strands at the other end of the electroscopes became charged or not? How do you know?

Use the diagrams below to show your thinking about the +/– charged entities on the **charged acrylic sheet, the soda can, the water bottle, and the tinsel**, both before and after they have been in contact.

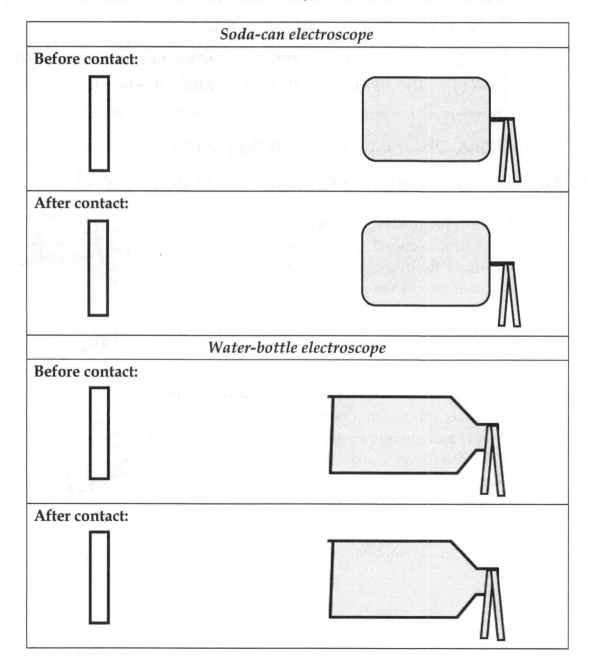

| *Soda-can electroscope* |
| **Before contact:** |
| **After contact:** |
| *Water-bottle electroscope* |
| **Before contact:** |
| **After contact:** |

🧩 Explain, in terms of the +/− charged entities involved, what you think happened when the acrylic sheet was touched to the base of both electroscopes and why the tinsel behaved as it did.

Participate in the class vote and discussion about this question.

CQ 4-1: According to your diagrams, after the positively (+) charged acrylic sheet was in contact with the base of the soda can and the water bottle, how were the tinsel strands at the other end of each electroscope charged, if at all?
  A. The tinsel on both was uncharged.
  B. The tinsel on the soda can was positively (+) charged. The tinsel on the water bottle was uncharged.
  C. The tinsel on the soda can was negatively (−) charged. The tinsel on the water bottle was uncharged.
  D. The tinsel on both was negatively (−) charged.
  E. The tinsel on both was positively (+) charged.

Now consider how your response to CQ 4-1 could be checked by making some predictions.

❓ If the tinsel on both electroscopes was charged according to your chosen response, how would it behave when a + charged acrylic sheet and a − charged Styrofoam plate were brought near to it? Fill in the prediction table and briefly discuss your reasoning with your group.

Prediction Table: What do you think would happen to the tinsel if the ... were brought near the ...? Choose _Attract_, _Repel_ or n_O_thing.

Brought near the tinsel	Tinsel on **soda-can** electroscope	Tinsel on **water-bottle** electroscope
Positively (+) charged acrylic		
Negatively (−) charged Styrofoam		

Watch a movie **(USE L4 Movie 2)** where the base end of the soda can and water bottle electroscopes were touched by the + charged acrylic sheet (not shown in movie), and then a charged acrylic sheet and charged Styrofoam plate are separately brought close to (but not touching) the tinsel strands on both electroscopes.

🔍 Fill in your observations in the table.

Observation Table: **What actually happened to the tinsel when the ... were brought near the ...?** **Choose** _A_*ttract,* _R_*epel or n*_O_*thing.*

	Tinsel on **_soda-can_** electroscope	Tinsel on **_water-bottle_** electroscope
Positively (+) charged acrylic		
Negatively (−) charged Styrofoam		

After the acrylic sheet was in contact with the base of the metal soda can, were the tinsel strands positively (+) or negatively (−) charged, or were they still uncharged? How do you know?

After the acrylic sheet was in contact with the base of the plastic water bottle, were the tinsel strands positively (+) or negatively (−) charged, or were they still uncharged? How do you know?

If these outcomes do not agree with your predictions, discuss with your group how you could modify your thinking about the mobility of the charged entities in different materials to account for it.

Describe your current thinking about why the metal soda can and the plastic soda bottle produced different results in these experiments.

Part 2: How can charged materials be discharged?

You have seen how uncharged objects can become charged, either by rubbing them together (or peeling apart, in the case of the tapes) or by touching them with another object that is already charged. Now we will consider how we can turn a charged object into an uncharged object, a process called *discharging*.

Suppose you have a soda-can electroscope and a water-bottle electroscope. You charge the tinsel strands on both by touching them directly with a positively (+) charged acrylic sheet. You have already seen that this would cause the tinsel strands to themselves become positively (+) charged and hang in a more spread out pattern than before they were touched.

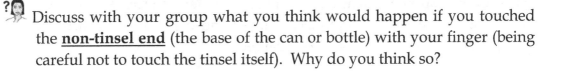 Discuss with your group what you think would happen if you touched the **non-tinsel end** (the base of the can or bottle) with your finger (being careful not to touch the tinsel itself). Why do you think so?

Participate in the class vote and discussion.

> **CQ 4-2: What would happen if you touched the non-tinsel end of a positively (+) charged soda can and water bottle electroscopes?**
> A. Both electroscopes would discharge.
> B. Only the soda can electroscope would discharge.
> C. Only the water bottle electroscope would discharge.
> D. Neither electroscope would discharge.

Watch a movie **(USE L4 Movie 3)** of the demonstation being performed. The tinsel on both electroscopes will be charged by allowing the strands to touch a positively (+) charged acrylic sheet. The demonstrator will then touch a finger to the non-tinsel end on both electroscopes. Watch the behavior of the tinsel when this is done. At the end, the demonstrator will allow the tinsel to touch some fingers directly.

Which of the electroscopes could be discharged by touching the non-tinsel end—only the water bottle, only the soda can, or both? Explain why you think this is in terms of the behavior of the +/− charged entities in the different materials involved.

Why do you think the tinsel on the water-bottle electroscope could be discharged by touching it directly with some fingers, but touching the bottle itself did not work?

Recall that the outer surface of the tinsel strands is a thin layer of metal. Now let's consider how we could discharge an object that has no metal anywhere on it. You know that, when rubbed together, the rubbed surface of an acrylic sheet becomes positively (+) charged and the rubbed surface of a Styrofoam plate becomes negatively (–) charged.

If you wanted to discharge these two objects again, do you think it would be sufficient to touch each of them at **only one point** on the charged surface, or would it be better to touch **as much of the rubbed surface as possible**? Explain your thinking in terms of your ideas about the behavior of the +/− charged entities in these non-metallic materials.

Watch a movie **(USE L4 Movie 4)** of both these ideas being tested. Whether the materials remain charged or not will be tested for using an **uncharged** soda can electroscope. (Recall that there is always an attraction between a charged and an uncharged object.)

What happened? Did touching either the charged acrylic or charged Styrofoam at **one point** discharge them, or did you need to **touch all over** their rubbed surfaces? If the result does not agree with your prediction, discuss with your group how you could change your thinking about the behavior of charged and uncharged objects.

Does the result does agree with your prediction? If not, discuss with your group how you could change your model (in terms of the behavior of charged entities in non-metals) to account for it.

In a previous lesson you saw a plastic stirrer being charged by being rubbed with wool and then touched all over with the fingers. After being touched, the stirrer was no longer charged. [If you need a reminder, watch the movie **(USE L4 Movie 5)** again.]

Assuming the rubbed plastic stirrer was negatively (–) charged, how can your model explain this result in terms of the behavior of the +/– charged entities involved?

Summarizing Questions

S1. As a result of the evidence you have seen in this lesson, you may have felt it necessary to revise your model so that it can account for the difference between how metals and non-metals behave when involved in static electric effects.

CQ 4-3: Which of the following best accounts for the difference between how metals and non-metals behave when involved in static electricity effects?

A. At least some of the charged entities can move around in non-metals, but not in metals.

B. At least some of the charged entities can move around in metals, but not in non-metals.

C. The charged entities in metals and non-metals are different and do not interact with each other.

S2. If you were to hold a brass rod in your hand and try to charge it by rubbing it with nylon, it would not work. However, if you were to wear thick rubber gloves, the brass rod would become charged. Briefly explain why this is.

S3. At this stage, your model probably accounts for an object being charged by assuming that it has more of one type of charge (+ or –) than the other.

> **CQ 4-4:** Do the observations you have made so far in this unit suggest that it would be better to regard the excess of one type of charged entity as lying on the surface of an object, or deep within the body of the object? Why do you think so?
> A. The excess of one type of charged entity lies on the surface.
> B. The excess of one type of charged entity lies deep within the body of the object.
> C. At this time, there is no evidence to decide.

S4. In this lesson you saw that when the base end of an uncharged soda can electroscope was **touched** with a positively (+) charged acrylic sheet, the tinsel at the other end also became positively (+) charged. Use the diagrams below to show how your current model can account for this in terms of the +/– charged entities involved.

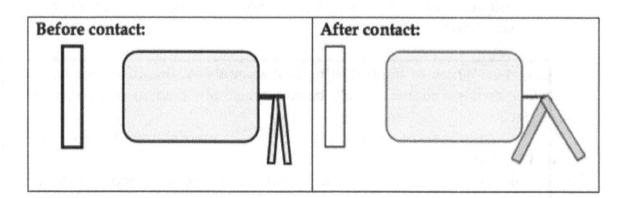

Before contact: **After contact:**

Conductors and insulators

Scientists refer to materials in which at least some charged entities can move around relatively freely as *conductors*. Materials for which none of the charged entities are free to move around are called *insulators*.

Purpose and Key Question

By now the class has likely reached consensus on a model of static electricity that should explain all the observations that have been made thus far. We refer to this model as the *charges in materials model*, and its basic **assumptions** are listed here. (1) Inside all objects there are two types of tiny charged entities, which we label + and −. The + charged entities are the protons in the nucleus of the atoms in the material and they cannot be easily removed or added to a material, or moved around. The − charged entities are the electrons that orbit around the nucleus and some of these can be removed or added to a material, and can move around to some degree. (2) In an uncharged material there are an equal number of + and − charges. An object is given an overall − charge when extra − charges are added to it. An object is given an overall + charge when some of its − charges are removed. The excess charges (+ or −) are on the surface of the material. (3) In metallic materials, some − charges are free to move throughout the body of the material. In non-metals, the − charges are not free to move through the material but stay attached to a particular atom. However, while staying attached to that atom they can be moved slightly with respect to the + charges in the nucleus.

In this lesson we will apply this model to explain some new observations.

> *How can you use the charges in materials model of static electricity to explain some phenomena?*

Predictions, Observations and Making Sense

Part 1: Can a charged object pick up small, uncharged objects?

You have seen that when a rubber balloon is rubbed on wool (or hair), it becomes negatively (−) charged. Suppose you rubbed a balloon on your hair, and then held it first above a pile of small pieces of aluminum foil (metal), and then held it above a pile of small pieces of paper (non-metal). Do you think the balloon would attract any of the pieces and so pick them up?

CQ 5-1: If you hold a negatively (−) charged balloon above some small pieces of aluminum and paper, what do you think would happen?

A. The balloon would not pick up anything.
B. The balloon would pick up some aluminum pieces, but no paper.
C. The balloon would pick up some paper pieces, but no aluminum.
D. The balloon would pick up both some paper and some aluminum pieces.

Why do you think so?

Watch a movie (USE L5 Movie) so you can test your prediction.

Which pieces does the balloon pick up: neither, only one type, or both?

Now use the model of charges in materials to explain this result. First use the diagrams below (which are not to scale) to show the +/− charges on the balloon and one of the uncharged **aluminum** pieces, both when the negatively (−) charged balloon is far away and when it is closer.

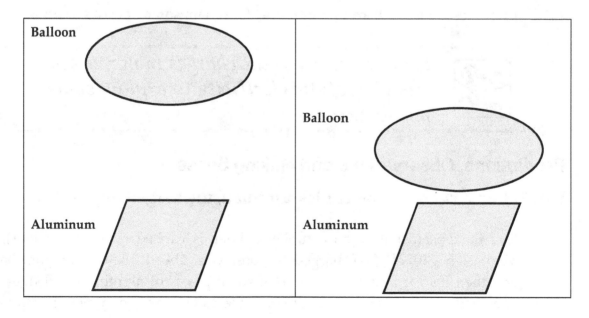

Explain what happened to the +/− charged entities in the aluminum piece when the negatively (−) charged balloon was brought close.

How does the arrangement of +/− entities in the aluminum piece explain why it is attracted to the balloon?

Now use the diagrams below to show the +/− charges on the balloon and one of the uncharged paper pieces both when the negatively (−) charged balloon is far away and when it is closer.

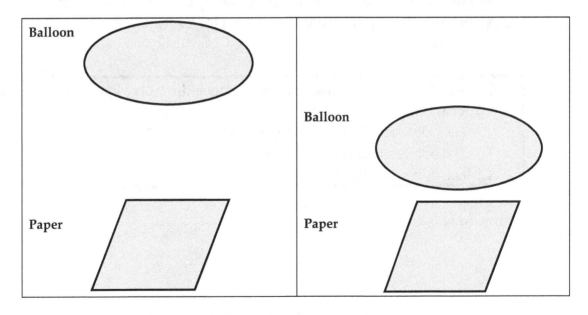

Explain what happened to the +/− charged entities in the paper piece when the negatively (−) charged balloon was brought close.

How does the arrangement of +/− entities in the paper piece explain why it is attracted to the negatively (−) charged balloon?

Part 2: How can you explain why clothes stick together in a dryer?

A student doing her laundry takes wet clothes from a washing machine and puts them in the dryer. When they are dry she takes them out and finds a pair of cotton socks stuck to a polyester shirt because of 'static cling'. Wondering what has happened to cause this, she does a quick experiment using a balloon hanging from string (left over from the previous night's party!). She rubs the balloon on her hair and then lets it hang freely from the string. When she brings the clothes near to the balloon, she finds it is attracted to the cotton socks but repelled by the polyester shirt. However, she finds that the cotton socks repel each other.

CQ 5-2: What type of charge (+ or −) does the polyester shirt have, or is it uncharged?
  A. The polyester shirt is + charged.
  B. The polyester shirt is − charged.
  C. The polyester shirt is uncharged.

How do you know?

CQ 5-3: What type of charge (+ or −) do the cotton socks have, or are they uncharged?
  A. The cotton socks are both + charged.
  B. The cotton socks are both − charged.
  C. One cotton sock is + charged; the other is − charged.
  D. The cotton socks are both uncharged.

How do you know?

Use the charges in materials model to explain what happened to the cotton socks and polyester shirt during drying. Draw + and – entities on the diagrams below.

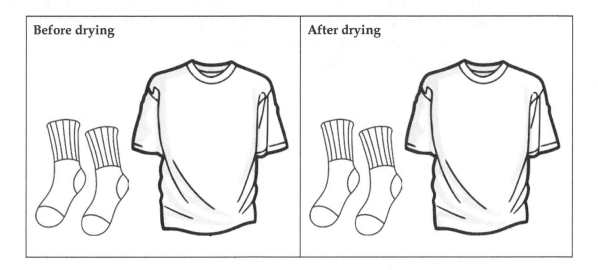

Explain what happens to the cotton socks and polyester shirt during drying.

When the student checked on her laundry halfway through the drying cycle, it was still slightly damp, but there was also no 'static cling' evident. Why do you think this was?

To reduce 'static cling', you can put a 'dryer sheet' in the dryer with your laundry. These sheets coat the fibers of all your clothes with the same waxy substance as it tumbles with them. How might this substance work to reduce the 'static cling'?

ISBN 978-1-68231-338-1

9 781682 313381 >

Activate
Learning®